Action Sports Library

FREESTYLE WATER SKIING

Bob Italia

Published by Abdo & Daughters, 6535 Cecilia Circle, Edina, Minnesota 55439.

Library bound edition distributed by Rockbottom Books, Pentagon Tower, P.O. Box 36036, Minneapolis, Minnesota 55435.

Copyright ©1993 by Abdo Consulting Group, Inc., Pentagon Tower, P.O. Box 36036, Minneapolis, Minnesota 55435. International copyrights reserved in all countries. No part of this book may be reproduced in any form without written permission from the publisher.

Printed in the United States.

Library of Congress Cataloging - in - Publication Data

Italia, Robert, 1955-
    Free style water skiing / Bob Italia.
        p.   cm. -- (Action sports)
    Includes bibliographical references and index.
    Summary: Introduces water skiing, a diverse water sport which has witnessed many changes since it began in 1922.
    ISBN 1-56239-232-8
    1. Water skiing -- Juvenile literature.   [1. Water skiing.]
I. Title.   II. Series
GV840.S5I85   1993
797.3 '5 -- dc20   93-19135
                                                          CIP
                                                           AC

Cover Photo: Allsport.
Inside Photos: Adventure Photo 11.
        Allsport 4, 7, 8, 13, 14, 15, 19, 21, 23, 28.
        SportsChrome, Inc. 8, 24.

Warning: The series *Action Sports Library* is intended as entertainment for children. These sporting activities should never be attempted without the proper conditioning, training, instruction, supervision, and equipment.

Edited by Rosemary Wallner

CONTENTS

More Than Just Water Skiing 5

Skiing On 8-Foot Skis 5

Gearing Up 10

Let's Go Skiing 16

Slalom Skiing 18

The Slalom Course 20

Trick Skiing 22

Kneeboarding 25

The Jump Ramp 27

Water Ski Tournaments 30

Glossary 32

Freestyle water skiing is pure fun.

FREESTYLE WATER SKIING

More Than Just Water Skiing

Freestyle water skiing has come a long way since the early days of water sports. Today, many fun and exciting variations of the sport exist. New equipment is developed each year. Whether you are looking for the thrills of a jump ramp, the challenge of a slalom course, or the spontaneous action of a kneeboard, freestyle water skiing has it all.

Skiing on 8-Foot Skis

Eighteen-year-old Ralph Samuelson was the first person to ride on a pair of water skis. He did it in Lake City, Minnesota, in 1922. Samuelson figured that if people could ski on snow, they could ski on water.

First, he tried to water ski on snow skis. When this didn't work, he tried narrow strips of wood from barrels. That didn't work either.

Determined to succeed, Samuelson made his own water skis out of pine boards. His skis were 8 feet long and 9 inches wide. He fastened them to his feet with leather straps. For a towrope, he used a long sash cord. The handle was a rubber-wrapped metal ring.

Once he had his equipment, Samuelson decided to give water skiing a try. Day after day, he tried to get up behind a 24-foot motor launch. But he found that starting was difficult. Finally, as the people of Lake City watched with curiosity, he succeeded.

Samuelson perfected his starting technique. Once he felt comfortable skiing on two skis, he developed some stunts. He learned to ski on one ski. Then he made a jump ramp. Greasing the ramp with lard, Samuelson performed the first water jumps.

News of Samuelson's accomplishments spread. Soon, he traveled the country, putting on his one-man daredevil show.

Water skiing remained a daredevil show until 1939. That's when Dan B. Hains organized the American Water Ski Association (AWSA). That year, the AWSA held its first National Water Ski Championships at Jones Beach State Park on Long Island, New York. The competition included slalom skiing, trick skiing, and jumping.

After World War II, affordable, higher-horsepower outboard engines became available to more and more people. Since Americans had more money to spend on leisure activities like boating, water skiing became a popular water sport.

From its humble beginnings, water skiing has become a diverse sport. Water ski enthusiasts continually invent new ways to have fun. Equipment and boats continue to improve.

Besides the common squared-back water skis, skiers use high-tech slalom skis, trick skis, kneeboards, discs, mini-surfboards, inflatable tubes, and other water toys. Skiing without any skis—known as barefooting—has also become popular.

Barefoot skiing

The three events of competition water skiing.

Slalom

Trick skiing

Jumping

Competition water skiing has developed into a major sporting event. Every year, ski tournaments attract thousands of fans. The tournaments consist of slalom skiing, trick skiing, and jumping—just as they did when competition skiing began.

Slalom skiers are racers. They zoom back and forth through a zigzagging slalom course of buoys. Trick skiers are dancers. They perform an entertaining program of twirling and skipping. Jump skiers are daredevils. They hurl themselves at high speed over a jump ramp, then arc gracefully through the air in a thrilling leap.

Show skiing has helped to increase water skiing's popularity. Show skiing can be found anywhere there are water skiing fans. These highly-entertaining shows are performed by amateur skiing clubs, or by professionals like the world famous Cypress Gardens skiers in Florida. Most shows offer some form of water ballet, wacky clown acts, water stunts, and amazing multi-tiered human pyramids.

Still another form of water skiing is freestyle skiing. Freestyle skiing combines trick skiing and jumping. The freestyle skier performs long distance flips, twirls, and other tricks off the jump ramp.

Whatever form of water skiing you choose, you'll be guaranteed thrills and excitement.

Gearing Up

Having the proper gear is important for all water skiers. The type of equipment you choose depends on your skill level and the kind of water skiing you will perform. Spending a little extra for good equipment is recommended. But don't buy anything that has features you may never need.

Choosing water skis can be difficult. Years ago, all water skis were made of wood. Now, skis come with many different features to fit the varieties of water skiing.

Most water skis are made of fiberglass with plastic foam cores. These skis are light, fast, and easy to maneuver and care for. Fiberglass skis last much longer than wooden skis. The best water skis have binders made of neoprene rubber or neoprene compounds. Binders are rubber boots on skis that hold the skier's foot in place. The neoprene rubber binders have thumb-screw adjustment devices. Vinyl binders are not recommended. They are hard and tear easily.

The four types of water skis are: combination pairs, slalom skis, trick skis, and jump skis. All ski types come in recreational, intermediate, and tournament models.

Combination pairs are the most popular type of water ski. Skiers use this type for two-ski recreational skiing or one-ski slalom skiing. One of the combination skis has double binders for slalom skiing. A double binder allows you to place two feet on one ski. When you are ready to slalom on one ski, you simply drop the ski with the single binder and use the double binder ski.

Slalom skis come in many models designed for different skill levels. If you're just learning to slalom, use a recreational slalom ski. It has a wide tail and a flat bottom. It makes starting easy and rises high and fast on the water.

A slalom ski has double-binders.

When you develop your slalom skills, you will make sharper turns and harder cuts. That's when you should switch to an intermediate slalom ski. An intermediate slalom ski has a tapered tail, beveled edges, and a concave bottom.

The tapered tail allows the skier to ride deeper in the water. The beveled edges help skiers slow down so they can make controlled turns. The concave bottom helps the skier hold the turn.

Intermediate skis come in three lengths. Skiers who weigh less than 125 pounds use the 64-inch ski. Skiers who weigh between 125 and 175 pounds use the 66-inch ski. Skiers who weigh more than 175 pounds use the 68-inch ski.

Tournament skis are designed for the difficult turns and cuts on a slalom course. But they are hard to start on and wobble when skiing straight ahead. Even worse, they're expensive. Only the best slalom skiers should use tournament skis.

Skiers who want to do water stunts use trick skis. Trick skis are short and wide without fins. They can turn and slide in any direction, allowing skiers to twirl and hop.

Freestyle Water Skiing • 13

Trick skis are short and wide without fins.

Jump skis are lightweight—and expensive.

Novice ramp jumpers should look at jump skis. But be ready to pay a high price for them. Jump skis are designed to be light, yet withstand incredible pounding. Because of their special construction, jump skis are expensive.

Towropes come in different lengths and construction. A standard water ski rope is 75 feet long and has one 12-inch handle. The recreational skier should buy either polyethylene or polypropylene ropes with wood or foam handles.

Skiers who plan on competitive water skiing need a stronger towrope made of 12-strand polypropylene. A competition towrope has a minimum break load of 1,300 pounds, and can withstand all the fast, hard turns a competition skier must perform.

Freestyle Water Skiing • 15

Ski vests are a must!

Trick skiers use a trick rope. Trick ropes are only 45 feet long. They are made of polyethylene, which does not stretch as much as polypropylene.

Ski vests are a must for every skier. Choose a Coast Guard approved vest made of foam covered with vinyl or nylon fabric. Both work well, but vinyl tends to crack. The vest should have three nylon straps that wrap completely around the chest. The straps should also have plastic buckles.

Wet suits are useful if you want to ski in cold weather or cold water. They are made of buoyant foam that soaks up water. Wet suits allow a thin film of water to build up next to the body. Body temperature heats the water and keeps you warm.

You can buy full-length wet suits, or shorty wet suits. Full-body wet suits cover you from your wrists to your ankles. Shorty wet suits have short legs and sleeves, and allow freer movement.

Shorty wet suit

For those who don't want to get wet, a dry suit is in order. A dry suit is made of rubberized fabric. It seals at the neck, wrists, and ankles, preventing water from entering the suit. Dry suits work well, but they are expensive and don't allow as much movement as wet suits. Whether you choose a wet or dry suit, always wear a ski vest over it.

Water ski gloves are recommended for the serious skier. They improve gripping power and lessen fatigue during turns. Gloves are made of vinyl or suede leather. The leather gloves are more expensive, but they last a lot longer.

Whatever equipment you buy, make sure you take care of it. Keeping the gear clean and dry after use will prolong its life, and make skiing safer.

Let's Go Skiing

To start in deep water on two skis, draw your knees to your chest and hunch your shoulders forward. Keep the skis close together but not touching. The tips should point from the water with the towrope between them. Extend your arms outside your knees and grip the handle at the ends. Wait until the towrope is fully extended. Now you're ready to yell, "Hit it!"

When the boat begins to pull you, lock yourself in the starting position until you are up and out of the water. Don't try to stand and don't pull the handle toward you. Let the boat pull you up as you keep your skis together.

Once the skis are out of the water and skimming the surface, keep your weight back, knees bent, arms extended, and skis close together. Keep your back straight. Don't lean forward. Leaning forward will make it more difficult to ski.

When you feel comfortable skiing forward, try skiing over the wake. Lean in the direction you want to ski, keeping your weight back and your skis together. Cross the wake at an angle and don't slow down. If you lose momentum, you won't be able to cross the wake.

Once outside the wake, you will find yourself in calm water. Now you can practice turning and cutting. If you encounter another boat wake, lean back farther and bend your knees to absorb the shock.

When you have skied enough, it is easy to stop. Just let go of the handle and glide across the surface until you slow down and sink into the water. Never land too close to a dock, pier, or the shoreline. And watch for other boats, skiers, or swimmers. It is best to land in deeper water away from any trouble, then swim in.

Slalom Skiing

Once you have mastered water skiing on two skis, you may want to try slalom skiing on one ski. Slalom skiing is difficult. But there is nothing like carving the water and sending up walls of spray.

Use a pair of combination skis. Practice lifting the single-binder ski out of the water for as long as you can. This will help you develop a sense of balance needed to ski on a single ski.

Keep your back erect and your knees bent. Now lift the single-binder ski off the water, keeping the tip up and your eyes forward. Hold the ski up longer each time you raise it in the air. When you can hold it up for five seconds or more, you're ready to drop the ski.

The binder of the drop ski should be loose so you can easily let it go. Instead of lifting it in the air, slide the ski back. Lift your heal from the binder and keep your weight on the ball of your foot still in the binder. Your skiing knee should be bent and your arms tucked in.

If you feel balanced, let the ski go by extending your leg and pointing you toes. Do this smoothly. Don't make any sudden movements that will upset your balance.

Slalom skiing

Now that your foot is free, hold it in the air or drag it in the water. Don't put it into the back binder of the slalom ski too quickly. Wait until you feel in control and balanced.

Once you feel comfortable, place your free foot on the ski as close to your front foot as possible. This allows you to find the rear binder. When you do, carefully slip your foot in, making sure it is fully inserted. Now put your weight on your back foot. If the ski wobbles, lean back farther and move your foot forward on the ski. Keep your back straight and knees bent.

To make turns, lean in the direction you want to go. Pull the handle toward your hip and keep your shoulders back. Your knees should be bent at all times.

The more you lean and the harder you pull, the faster you will go. In time, your turns will become sharper, and you will send a spray high into the air.

The Slalom Course

When you become comfortable with slalom skiing, you may want to try a slalom course. It consists of a corridor of six buoys. The ski boat passes through the corridor while the slalom skier must ski around the buoys in a zigzag fashion.

Skiing around buoys requires much accelerating and slowing down. And both must be done quickly. Approach the first buoy with a wide turn. Once around it, cut quickly across the boat wake and aim wide of the second buoy. This allows you to make a smooth, even turn. Continue this wide approach to the buoys to avoid the difficult, sharp turns. Skiing directly at the buoys will force you into difficult turns. Eventually, you will run out of room and miss a buoy.

The slalom course

Trick Skiing

Trick skiing has no set routines or courses to follow. The program is left up to the skier. It is by far the most creative form of water skiing. Some of the most popular tricks include sideslides and surface turns.

Skiers perform sideslides by turning the trick skis perpendicular to the ski boat so that the skiers are sliding sideways.

To perform a sideslide, you must turn the skis fully perpendicular to the boat. Turning part of the way will cause the skis to run toward the wake. Eventually, the skis will slide from under you.

Begin the sideslide by keeping your back straight, knees bent, and handle pulled close. Now swivel your hips and turn the skis so they are perpendicular to the boat. Hold the handle close to your hip and spread the skis apart, leaning away from the boat to keep the forward edges up. Hold the slide position by keeping your back erect and knees bent. Return to the forward position, turn so the handle is in front of you.

Freestyle Water Skiing • 23

The sideslide

Surface turns allow you to ski backwards. Begin a surface turn by pulling the handle close to your waist. Now rotate your hips and knees, releasing the outside hand as you turn. Don't hesitate while making the turn. Make sure you keep the handle close and keep your skis together.

Surface turns

Now that your back is facing the boat, swing your free hand around and grab the handle. Keep your back erect and your eyes forward. Ski backwards for a while for practice. To return forward, let go with one hand while keeping the handle close. The towrope will pull you around. Regrasp the handle quickly before it is pulled away from your body.

Kneeboarding

Kneeboarding is the most popular novelty ski on the water today. A kneeboard is short, wide, and shaped like a football. It has a padded top and is designed to be ridden in a kneeling position.

It does not take a lot of power to pull a kneeboard. You can make sharp cuts, jump wakes, spin, and flip on a kneeboard. And they're easy to get up on.

Lie on the board with your legs extended behind you. Grasp both sides of the board and pull it beneath you. Then move as far forward as you can while keeping the nose of the board up.

Now grab the handle of the towrope and hold it near the nose of the board. Make sure you are propped up on your elbows. Tell the driver to "Hit it!" Lean back to keep the nose of the board up.

When the board begins to level off, shift your weight forward to your elbows. Bring your knees up under you and slowly sit up. As you continue your ride, grab the knee strap with one hand and hold it up. Then slide your knees under it before securing the strap. Most straps have Velcro fasteners that make it easy to secure. But don't pull the strap too tight.

Now you're ready to cut from side to side. Lean in the direction you want to go while pulling the handle to your hip. When you feel comfortable making cuts, try jumping the boat wake. The nose of the board will bounce when it hits the wake, so keep your weight back and hold on tight. Make sure the nose stays out of the water when you land. Otherwise, you will tumble.

Once you have mastered the wake, try some turnarounds. Lean forward and extend the handle. Now use your legs and knees to turn the board. Hold onto the towrope with one hand and pull the handle toward you as you turn, leaning away from the boat. Leaning away will keep the edge of the board out of the water. Once you are completely turned around, regrasp the handle with your free hand.

To return to a forward position, lean away from the boat and turn with your legs and knees, holding the handle close with one hand. When you are facing forward, keep your weight back and regrasp the handle with your free hand.

Kneeboarding is a fun and exciting water sport. The more you practice, the better you will become.

The Jump Ramp

Jumping over a ramp on water skis sounds scary. But with the proper technique and practice, ramp jumping can be the most thrilling and rewarding of all water sports.

A ramp jumper must be confident and strong on two skis. Having the proper equipment is also a must. Besides jump skis and a 75-foot towrope, a jumper needs a pair of wet suit shorts and a helmet designed for water ski jumps.

A jump ramp is 14 feet wide and 22 feet long above the water. It has an adjustable waxed plywood deck and plywood safety aprons on the sides.

Beginners should always jump on calm days. Wet the ramp surface and set the ramp at 5 feet. Then attempt a corner jump.

A corner jump is performed by skiing over the lower right hand corner of the ramp. Approach the ramp at a 30 to 40 degree angle. Make contact with the ramp's right corner about 2 feet up. Keep your skis together and flat. Otherwise, they will slip out from under you, and you will tumble. Your back should be erect and your knees bent. Your weight should be slightly forward. Make sure the handle is pulled close to your waist and your elbows are tucked into your hips.

28 • *Action Sports Library*

The jump ramp

Once you are airborne, keep your tips in the air and lock in the jump position. When you land, absorb the shock with your legs. Bend your knees, but don't let them collapse.

Try a bigger jump each time you approach the ramp. The more you jump, the more confident you will become. Soon, you will be ready to go over the top.

To jump over the top, aim for the lower left corner of the ramp. As you approach the ramp, it may look like a solid wall. But it only takes a second to fly over it.

Ski diagonally from the lower left corner to the upper right corner. Then lock yourself in the jump position: knees bent, skis together, weight forward. When you zoom off the top, you will feel like you're floating. Then you will begin to drop.

Maintain the jump position and keep your skis together with the tips up. Hold the handle at your waist, even though the towrope is slack. Don't look down or your tips will drop. Keep your eyes on the boat.

Land with your weight on the balls of your feet. Landing on your heels will cause you to tumble. Hold on tight to the handle with both hands so it isn't pulled away when the towrope tightens.

Don't be discouraged if your first full ramp jump isn't successful. After a few tries, you should ski away from the ramp victoriously.

Water Ski Tournaments

Most freestyle water skiing enthusiasts ski for fun. But if you have mastered the slalom course, trick skiing, or the jump ramp, you may want to test your skills against others. To do this, you must join the American Water Ski Association (AWSA). They will supply you with a tournament schedule, addresses of ski clubs, tournament rules, and an AWSA membership card. You will need the card to enter tournaments.

Attend a few tournaments to see what they're like. When you feel ready to compete, look for a tournament that has a novice division for your particular event. To enter, obtain an official entry form and submit it before the deadline. You must also pay an entry fee and sign a responsibility waiver, releasing the tournament sponsors from any liability in the event of an accident. If you are a minor, a parent or guardian must sign for you.

When the day of the tournament arrives, get there early. You will need to fill out more forms. Then check in with the dock starter. The starter will safety check your equipment and obtain information about your skiing requirements such as the length of towrope you want to use and how fast you want the ski boat to go.

When your turn to compete arrives, relax and have fun. You may not win your event. You may even fall. But if you are persistent and practice hard, one day you will walk away with a trophy.

For more information about water skiing and other water sports, write to:

American Water Ski Association
P.O. Box 191
Winter Haven, FL 33882

GLOSSARY

Apron—the angled plywood on the sides of a water ski jump ramp.

AWSA—American Water Ski Association.

Barefooting—to water ski without skis.

Bevel—the rounded edge of a ski.

Binder—the rubber boot on a ski that holds the skier's foot.

Buoy—a floating object that is anchored in water.

Combination Pair—a pair of recreational water skis, one of which is used for slalom skiing.

Concave—the curved bottom of a ski.

Corner Jump—to ski over the lower corner of a jump ramp.

Freestyle Skiing—a type of water skiing where skiers perform tricks off the jump ramp.

Novice—a beginner.

Slalom—to ski in a zigzag pattern on a single ski.

Towrope—a rope with a handle that attaches to a boat; the skier hold onto the towrope as the boat pulls him or her through the water.

Wake—the waves produced by a moving boat.